D1252476

ULTIMATE COMICS
SPIDER-MAN

WRITER: **BRIAN MICHAEL BENDIS**

ARTIST, #16.1: **DAVID MARQUEZ**

ARTIST, #19-22: **SARA PICHELLI**

COLOR ARTIST: **JUSTIN PONSOR**

LETTERER: **VC'S CORY PETIT**

COVER ART: **DAVID MARQUEZ** & **JUSTIN PONSOR** (#16.1),
SARA PICHELLI & **RAINIER BEREDO** (#19 & #21-22) AND
SARA PICHELLI & **CHRISTINA STRAIN** (#20)

ASSISTANT EDITORS: **EMILY SHAW** & **JON MOISAN**

EDITOR: **MARK PANICCIA**

COLLECTION EDITOR: **JENNIFER GRÜNWALD**

ASSISTANT EDITORS: **ALEX STARBUCK** & **NELSON RIBEIRO**

EDITOR, SPECIAL PROJECTS: **MARK D. BEAZLEY**

SENIOR EDITOR, SPECIAL PROJECTS: **JEFF YOUNGQUIST**

SVP OF PRINT & DIGITAL PUBLISHING SALES: **DAVID GABRIEL**

EDITOR IN CHIEF: **AXEL ALONSO**

CHIEF CREATIVE OFFICER: **JOE QUESADA**

PUBLISHER: **DAN BUCKLEY**

EXECUTIVE PRODUCER: **ALAN FINE**

PREVIOUSLY:

MILES FOUND OUT THAT HIS FATHER AND HIS UNCLE AARON USED TO BE CRIMINALS. HIS DAD REFORMED BUT HIS UNCLE BECAME A WORLD-CLASS CRIMINAL KNOWN AS THE PROWLER. UNCLE AARON CONFRONTED MILES WITH THE TRUTH AND CONVINCED MILES TO JOIN HIM IN TAKING DOWN A REAL SUPER VILLAIN...THE SCORPION.

MILES REALIZED THAT HIS UNCLE WAS USING HIM, AND THEY HAD A CONFRONTATION THAT TURNED VIOLENT. UNCLE AARON DIED WHEN HIS BATTLESUIT BACKFIRED. THIS ALL HAPPENED IN FRONT OF A CROWD.

DURING THE BOLD ATTACKS OF A GRASSROOTS TERRORIST MILITIA KNOWN AS HYDRA THAT HAD DECLARED WAR ON THE STATUS QUO, MILES'S FATHER WAS TAKEN INTO S.H.I.E.L.D. CUSTODY ONLY TO BE RESCUED BY HYDRA. THEY HANDED HIM A GUN AND ASKED HIM TO JOIN THEIR REVOLUTION. HE, IN TURN, ATTACKED THEM AND RAN AWAY.

SPIDER-MAN BY BRIAN MICHAEL BENDIS VOL. 4. Contains material originally published in magazine form as ULTIMATE COMICS SPIDER-MAN #16.1 and #19-22. First printing 2013. ISBN#
. Published by MARVEL WORLDWIDE, INC., a subsidiary of MARVEL ENTERTAINMENT, LLC. OFFICE OF PUBLICATION: 135 West 50th Street, New York, NY 10020. Copyright © 2012 and 2013
nc. All rights reserved. All characters featured in this issue and the distinctive names and likenesses thereof, and all related indicia are trademarks of Marvel Characters, Inc. No similarity between
aaracters, persons, and/or institutions in this magazine with those of any living or dead person or institution is intended, and any such similarity which may exist is purely coincidental. **Printed**
N FINE, EVP - Office of the President, Marvel Worldwide, Inc. and EVP & CMO Marvel Characters B.V.; DAN BUCKLEY, Publisher & President - Print, Animation & Digital Divisions; JOE QUESADA,
r; TOM BREVOORT, SVP of Publishing; DAVID BOGART, SVP of Operations & Procurement, Publishing; C.B. CEBULSKI, SVP of Creator & Content Development; DAVID GABRIEL, SVP of Print & Digital
1 O'KEEFE, VP of Operations & Logistics; DAN CARR, Executive Director of Publishing Technology; SUSAN CRESPI, Editorial Operations Manager; ALEX MORALES, Publishing Operations Manager;
Emeritus. For information regarding advertising in Marvel Comics or on Marvel.com, please contact Niza Disla, Director of Marvel Partnerships, at ndisla@marvel.com. For Marvel subscription
800-217-9158. **Manufactured between** 5/20/2013 and 7/1/2013 by R.R. DONNELLEY, INC., SALEM, VA, USA.

FLLOOM

Oh my God!

You are...

just...

...like me.

What? **What** did you say?

They're calling someone.

Hold on.

You are...

just...

...like me.

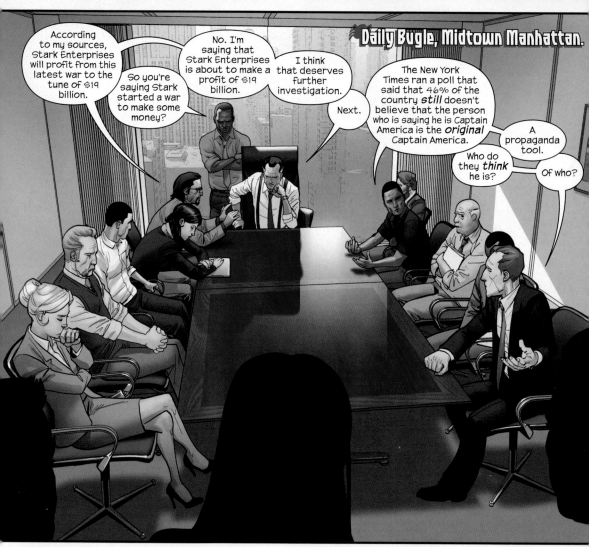

According to my sources, Stark Enterprises will profit from this latest war to the tune of $19 billion.

So you're saying Stark started a war to make some money?

No. I'm saying that Stark Enterprises is about to make a profit of $19 billion.

I think that deserves further investigation.

Next.

The New York Times ran a poll that said that 46% of the country *still* doesn't believe that the person who is saying he is Captain America is the *original* Captain America.

A propaganda tool.

Who do they *think* he is?

Of who?

I'm not running that.

Does anybody have anything that even slightly resembles an interesting take on an interesting story?

This country almost collapsed in civil war and none of you have anything interesting to write about?

I have something on this new Spider-Man.

Is it good?

This is amateur footage of the fight between Spider-Man and who the F.B.I. called The Prowler.

Now The Prowler's real name is--was Aaron Davis.

He was a cat burglar of some report, hence the name.

Before that just low-level, all-around scum his entire life.

But what's interesting is how crazy he got just about the same time this new Spider-Man popped up in our lives.

He started wearing gear and challenging the big dogs.

He's reportedly the one who took out *The Scorpion.*

That's true.

Spider-Man was there.

That's my point.

There is *some connection* between The Prowler and this new Spider-Man.

It looks like they were partnered up and then things went sour.

And if you can--well you can't hear but just before he dies...

He says something like:

You are...

just...

...like me.

And?

And if you look, see, you can see the new Spider-Man, he might be African-American.

What does *that* mean?

I think they might be related.

All my life.

How long have you lived in New York, Miss Brant?

And am I the first person to tell you that not all African-American people are related?

Thank you for that, Robbie.

But no.

There's a familiarity here. Between these two.

I think they *knew* each other very well.

I think they might be related.

I don't know.

I just think the country almost cracked itself in half under the foot of civil war.

I think there are bigger things to write about.

Well good for me that you aren't the editor-in-chief of this newspaper, Urich.

You're just a reporter like me and I don't have to ask *you* what I should be writing about.

Whatever you are looking for, you don't have it yet.

Don't come back into this room with nothing.

Don't come at me with something I can see on YouTube.

45 minutes till we lock the late edition.

Go!!

Are we really looking to out the new Spider-Man?

What is the story *about*?

A master criminal has a connection of some sort to this new Spider-Man.

We don't know anything about him.

You told me you go poking around and I think there is something here.

So the death of Peter Parker taught us nothing?

I was guarding her!! That's all I was doing!!

Officer Maddox.

Wow. Betty Brant.

You'd better not let my captain see you around here after that thing you wro--

I need a favor.

Wow.

A favor I will gladly return.

You have gigantic caliyoodas.

I'm desperate.

Please, John, I promise I will make it up to you.

You are going to get me fired.

I just need to see The Prowler file.

He's dead.

Then what could the harm possibly be?

Brooklyn, New York.

It was the strangest thing.

One day he's living here and the next day he just isn't.

He packed up in the middle of the night and just disappeared.

Still had 3 weeks left on his rent.

I certainly don't mind money for nothin'.

I'm just sayin' it was the strangest thing.

Usually we have to kick people out for *not* paying.

What's the rent?

$2,200 a month.

I'll take it.

Great. I'll go get the paperwork.

I'll be right back.

Great.

Great.

AH!

That is the biggest spider I have ever seen.

And it's not--it's not a tarantula.

Is it?

Gonna vomit.

So it's all pretty standard.

We will need first and last months rent plus a couple of--

Uh...

Hello?

ROXXON INDUSTRIES

You didn't call me back, Doctor Marcus.

Ah!

You should know me well enough to know not calling me back is not going to make me go away.

Go to hell, Betty.

Seriously, *straight* to hell.

I need your help.

I need *you* to go to hell.

I just need you to--

My interest in what you need after the way you--

What *is* this?

Where did you *get* that?

You *know* what this is.

Where did you *get* that??!!

Let *go* of me!!

Where did you get it??!!

I found it!!

God!!

Was it dead when you found it?

It looks like it's been dead for a long time.

Look at *that.*

It calcified.

You've seen this before?

Yes, I have.

This--this was part of a project I was working on.

You? Here?

No. Oscorp. This was a while ago.

Oscorp? What does that number mean?

I tell you and my name ends up in another one of your hatchet job rag--

The only way I promise to keep your name *out* of it is you tell me what it is.

Like I can trust--

I promise!

Do you remember Spider-Man?

The original one?

Well, Peter Parker, it seems, was bit by a spider that was being genetically experimented on at Oscorp.

Once Norman Osborn found out *he* accidentally invented Spider-Man...he spent the rest of *his* life trying to duplicate that experiment.

He literally *killed* himself trying to do it.

This was test subject 42.

Where did you *find* it?

Did it go missing or was it stolen?

What do you want for it?

It's not for sale.

Are you saying *this* spider could give someone Spider-Man powers?

Seriously, where did you get it?

No.

Osborn was *never* able to duplicate the process.

The Oz formula was a *complete* failure.

You can read about *that* online.

It's not a secret, Betty. S.H.I.E.L.D. raided the laboratories.

Maybe the spider got loose during the chaos.

Wait, hold on...

Could *this* spider have given that *new* Spider-Man spider-powers?

Did the process work after all?

Hey!! Come back here!!

Oh, you *complete* nightmare!! User!!

Oh please, that movie was the *worst*.

It was a masterpiece.

What??

When you're older you'll see that--

I'll pay you two to stop.

Brooklyn, New York.

How much?

Gotcha.

Well, I just became a very rich woman.

You don't say.

I know who the new Spider-Man is. I have physical evidence. I have proof. It's a great story. And I want you and I, right now, to work out our financial differences.

We have financial differences?

I don't like how much I make.

I don't like that I'm treated like a lesser reporter because of past indiscretions.

And I would like to rectify all of this in exchange for this world-wide exclusive.

Let me see it.

His name is Jefferson Davis.

He is Aaron Davis aka The Prowler's *brother.*

They got their hands on a genetically altered spider, the same kind that bit a young Peter Parker, and they teamed up for a while.

But they had a falling out and now one of them is dead.

I can read.

I'm not going to run this.

What?? It's *gold!!*

Okay, the world finds out this man is Spider-Man, which by the way, based on your prior record I'm not convinced is true...

You put that out there...*then* what?

Then the city has one less hero and this family's life is ruined.

The world will not be better.

Justice will not have been done.

You're just burying someone so you can...your words: make money.

You're *not* going to run this story?

No.

Well then I will *find* someone who will.

I'm sure you will.

You're *out* of your mind.

It's not a story.

It's-- what?

Then what *is* it??

Words *mean* something, Brant.

These words you're writing don't illuminate the truth.

They just-- all you're going to do is *ruin* a man.

Ruin his family.

I don't even know what you're *talking* about.

Everything that you've been through in your life, everything this city has been through... and you learned *nothing*?

That makes you a fool.

One of us will sleep very well tonight.

You bet!!

How much do you think I could get?

Really? No, I-I got it.

I got the *actual* spider that gave him his powers. I have it *in* my possession.

I have it on me *now*.

This is a *huge* relief. This is *great* news.

Ned Leeds told me what an amazing job you did getting him his book deal.

I should've done this *years* ago.

Really? *Letterman??*

If you can make *that* happen I will *marry* you!

Ha! Okay, great.

You got my number.

Thank you *so* much.

And you can officially suck it, you Hitler mustache-wearing--

Trying to profit off of things that don't belong to you.

Oh my God!!

Please, whatever it is that you--

CHUCK

Ggkk!

VENOM WAR

The Northern Spotted Owl is primarily...what?

Wood rats and flying squirrels. Yes, it's true.

I'M TOTALLY OUT.

But do not be fooled, the Northern Spotted Owl will also eat other small animals.

I SO GOT THIS.

Give it up, Ganke.

What?

The phone.

What phone?

Ganke.

Yes.

Ganke?

What

What can I do for you...? Detective...?

Detective Maria Hill.

Homicide.

This is about Betty Brant.

Yes, it is, Mr. Jameson.

Yes, it is.

Well, obviously, I will help you in any way I can.

Jonah, I think you should wait for your lawyer to get here.

I'm not *guilty* of anything, Robbie.

Guilty people need their lawyers present.

The woman is dead. I will help in any way I can.

And so will you.

She came to see you a couple of hours before the time of death...

Yes.

She was here about this time yesterday.

I'm sure my secretary has a log.

Do you remember what the conversation was about?

It wasn't pleasant.

Could you be more specific?

She said: I know who the new Spider-Man is. Who he really is.

She said: I have physical evidence. I have proof.

Slow *down*, Miles!

Hungry. Do they not *feed* you at that school??

Yesshh!

Slow down. It's not a race.

Miles' Parents' Apartment. Brooklyn, NY.

BBZZZ

Who is it?

Work.

You're not going to get it?

No.

BBZZZ

KNOCK KNOCK

Who is here?

I have it.

KNOCK KNOCK

Please, Mr. Davis, we just want to get your side of the story...

Damn it.

Ow! My
back!!

You're on
a kid!

Yeah, uh,
could you
get off me,
please!?

Why didn't you
tell me this was
happening?

24-
hour news
cycle.

It's a
24-hour news
cycle.

It'll
go away in
24 hours.

Why won't
you talk to
them and be
done with
it?

Come
on...

Wait,
what did
you do?

I'm sorry,
boy.
Sorry
you had to
see that.

You fought
HYDRA??!!

I did
too.

We--we
have that in
common.

Kind
of.

Hey man, all we needed was 14 seconds of B roll for the 11 o'clock and if that's the 14 seconds--

Uh-oh. Hey, he's here.

Oh, hey, change your mind?

All we want to do is get you on record. Tell your story.

Who told you where I live?

I looked it up--we, yeah, we looked it up.

I'm *unlisted*. As in: *not* listed!

Who told you where I live??

Buddy, listen, we're trying to--all we are trying to do is run a piece about a local man who rose up and acted like a hero.

Why are *you* acting like I just caught you stealing a handful of Slim Jims at the--

Who told you *where* I live??!!

I don't think I appreciate your--*holy!*

Oh my god!

What the...?

SSSSSSS

20

Oh!! What *is* that? Whoa!! Your dad-- he's-- Being attacked *by a monster*??!! Go. What *is* that??

Talk *later!!* Go! Throw your mask on and go!!

Do you even know who I am?? I wonder.

Here, hey, wait, I did it. This is why I came over. I have more web fluid for you!! I made it!

Call the police!!

What *is* that monster thing? It looks familiar!

I'm calling *The Hulk!*

Gragghh!!

Uh, sir, you must get up out of the street!!

What--what is that? What is *happening?!*

Just *go!!*

What voice am I doing?

An *English accent??* Idiot!

He's going to figure out I'm his son.

He's going to see right through this.

He's not stupid.

Tell me you're getting this!

I just peed.

Oh my dear lord.

Wait, this--I know where I saw this!!

Peter Parker fought this thing!

I'm confused.

You're confused?

How did it end up here in front of *my* house??

Ok, so Spider-Man *isn't* who I thought he was!

You *are* much shorter in person...

Let's see who *you* really are.

Wait, what?

He thought *who* was Spider-Man?

Heck with it. Just shut him down.

SHPACK

Arghh!

This...

...this also looked more impressive on TV.

DRIP

Oops.

Ganke.

Now you are desperately annoying me!!!

I came here for a reason and I'm not leaving until I do what I came here to do!!

Now all I have to do is figure out how to stop this before he blurts out my name, kills my family, or kills me!!

SMAASSHH

Haarrghh!

Whoa!   Jefferson!!

WAP

WHACK

No!

Okay, didn't see that--OW!

Okay, maybe it's time we tried a little Venom blast.

ZAAATTTT

I have to stop forgetting I can do that.

Got to get back and help my mom before--

Agh!

Ev-everybody freeze!!

DOWN ON THE GROUND!!

We need backup!!

Dispatch, do you read??!!!

BAM BAM BAM BAM BAM BAM

BAM

BAM BAM

Shooting??!! Just wait a sec and see if my venom blast does anything.

Come here so I can--wait--

What--

What did you just--

NO!

Oh man.

Okay, patient unresponsive, breathing irregularly at a rate of 2/min--

Call Brooklyn medical and tell them we are on our way.

No. Nonono...

Pinpoint pupils.

SpO2 of 86% on 2L.

Are you related to him, ma'am?

His wife. I'm his wife.

You can ride along *with* us.

Get ALS rolling.

We should wait till we get to the hospital.

We might not have time.

Ganke, I told you to go home.

I--

Where's Miles?

I--you-- you told him to stay in the house.

I'm right here, mom.

Dad?

Severe, blunt head trauma.

Apenic oxygenation.

Dude, ETCO2 tells you nothing about oxygenation.

I don't like the way he fell.

Spider-Man slapped him?

We'll get the statement on the way.

Do we really *need* another Spider-Man?

Go. Go home with Ganke.

Listen to my words.

I'm coming with you.

Mom, I--

You *listen!!*

21

VENOM WAR

Brooklyn.

Uggghh!

May I help you?

Fi-nally! I'll have the biggest hot chocolate that exists on the *planet*. I don't care if you have to go back there and get a bucket full of--

Mary Jane Watson?

Hey, Gwen. You *work* here?

Kinda. Hey, a job is a job.

You look good. How come you don't ever call me back?

Did you call?

Like, *weeks* ago but after you never called me back I kinda got the hint.

I've been busy.

Are you *mad* at me?

Can we not do this here?

Is it about Peter, because--?

I really don't want to...

Oh no.

SPIDER-MAN BROOKLYN MONSTER ATTACK

TURN ON THE SOUND!!

I don't know how.

Dave?

We have *customers*, Ms. Watson.

LOCAL HERO BEATEN IN FRONT OF FAMILY

Oh man, is that--?

That *is* him, isn't it?

That thing attacked him at his home?

You have *a* line!!

Ugh!!

That kid has *no idea* what he's doing.

Where are you going?

I'm going to go *help* him.

Hello?? Miss Watson??

I'm not paying you to stare off into space!!

You're barely paying me anyhow.

Wait up!!

Morales Apartment.
Brooklyn, NY.

Detective Hill, good.

We need you over here.

Is Spider-Man still around?

No, ma'am.

That monstery goo thing he was fighting?

Oh no. He--it disappeared.

Is anyone in pursuit?

Ma'am?

Pursuit. Where you chase after the bad guys.

It didn't exactly go down the way you--

Eyewitnesses?

A bunch of us on the job and we rounded up the civies over there.

Miles?

I don't see how this could possibly be your fault, Miles.

You don't see how a big Spider-Man villain showing up at my *front door* and beating my dad into *the hospital* could possibly be *my* fault?

(Man, I can't stop shaking...)

How did whatever that was know to come *here*?

I don't know.

What *is* that thing anyhow?

Ganke, I don't know.

Oh, hey, I found some YouTube footage of it, I think.

From just now?

No. No. From the Peter Parker, uh, era.

It's not very clear. It's kind of dark....

...but that's kinda the same thing, yeah?

With great power comes great responsibility.

What?

It's what Peter Parker used to say.

It's *why* he was Spider-Man.

But a day like this...I think it's the reason I'm *not* supposed to be Spider-Man!

This isn't your fault.

Instead of fighting that--that thing--I should have grabbed my mom and dad and swung them away from here and *saved* them.

Instead, I got into a fight that I had *no idea* if I could win or lose and *my dad*--!!

If you would've ran away with your mom and dad that thing would've *chased* you.

How is *that* a better plan?? You got that thing away from your parents as best you--

I'm going to the hospital!

Your mom told you *not* to.

Ganke, I know you're trying to *help* but--

There's nothing you can do there.

Maybe there is.

Hey, come on...remember when my dad died?

Remember how much help we were?

All they do at the hospital is tell you to *stay out of the way.*

And that doesn't mean your dad's gonna *die*, I'm just saying that we've been here before... we *know* what happens.

The best thing you can do is find out what this was and why they did it and how they know who you are...

...and shut it *down* before it happens again.

How?

I think we can help.

Everybody as a father. e died when Peter was a kid.

And he created *that* monster?

No.

He created a cure for cancer that *someone else* turned into this monster.

Peter's father would *never* let them use it for, like, the military or anything like that.

It *might* have been what got Peter's dad killed.

Do you know what a symbiote is? Ever hear the word?

Where did it come from and why was it here?

But he didn't attack *me*. He attacked my father.

Maybe he thinks *your father* is Spider-Man.

You have to tell him...

But then, thanks to Peter, thanks to a lot of things...

I was separated from it.

The part of it that was me got to be me again.

And here I am.

Now, I don't remember much of what I'm telling you.

I'm just repeating what Peter Parker told me.

She *was* dead.

This is an insane miracle.

I got a second chance.

A lot of people who came in contact with this thing were not so lucky.

So I'm telling you...

This fight you had tonight, with this thing...

It could have gone a lot worse.

What does it want from me?

Forget that...what is death like?

Infinite nothingness.

I knew it.

This *Venom* has a deep-rooted DNA genetic connection to the Parker bloodline.

It was originally created from Peter's father's DNA.

It literally stalked and hunted Peter once he...it realized who Peter was.

Now with Peter gone, it may just be looking for *you* because, like him, *you* became Spider-Man.

So whatever was special about Peter Parker genetically... you might have the same thing.

You were bit by a spider too.

Yeah... Yeah.

Just like Peter...

Peter was bit by a spider that was being genetically experimented on at--

Oscorp.

That's right.

That's where-- that's where the spider that bit me came from.

Now look at this! This *just* happened. Like, yesterday.

Someone broke into the long abandoned Oscorp laboratories and *destroyed it.*

Blew it all up.

WIN A 50G FORTUNE TODAY!

DAILY BUGLE

Oscorp's main facility destroyed

The exact same lab where Peter got bit by the spider.

I know. I was there when he got bit.

She was there.

You guys are freaking me out.

I'm having a good time.

Excuse me?

What is going on here exactly?

Wait, whoa, uh, you can't just come in here.

Get out of here before we call the--

I know you.

I am the detective working on your uncle's death case.

And now here I am again, Miles, because *your father* was attacked in *another* Spider-Man situation.

Wait, whoa, you can't just come in here.

You need a warrant. You need probable cause.

I love when *Law and Order* has a marathon and everyone thinks they know the--

Gwen Stacy. That's right.

Captain John Stacy was your dad.

My dad was a cop, genius.

Yeah.

My condolences. What happened to him I wouldn't wish on--

Yeah, great. You should leave.

I would but I can't help but wonder...

Peter Parker's ex-girlfriend and the girl who now lives in his house are here pow-wowing with *these* little boys all the way out here in *Brooklyn.*

Please-- please leave my house.

You're in a lot of trouble, young man. This thing that you fought tonight...

Two days ago, a reporter from the Daily Bugle, the paper where Peter Parker used to work...

She says she found out who the new Spider-Man really is.

Except she was murdered in her home.

Violently.

Traces of this *goo monster* all over her house.

Your uncle is dead, your father is in intensive care and murdering monsters are showing up on your front door.

Whatever you and your little pals here are up to, whatever you know...

I can't help you unless you let me.

Anything you want to share with me before someone *else* gets hurt... or worse?

S-someone was killed? For real?

We don't know *what* you're talking about and we don't have anything to say to you.

And my tablet takes great HD movies.

I'm making a movie right now of a police detective *breaking and entering* a private home and threatening minor children.

This isn't a game.

People are being hurt.

People are dying.

[REC]

That was nuts.

She's the police!

Kid, you were going to tell her what we know?

She could be *the Venom* for all we know.

Oh, yeah.

You all right, kid?

"What are you going to do?"

Rio Morales?

Me!! Me. That's me.

Come with me, please.

The doctor will talk to you about--

Is he okay?

Ma'am, I-- it's not my place.

Just tell me if he is okay!

Please tell me he's okay.

Aagghh!!

Holy!!

What the @#$@$@!!??

22

VENOM WAR

Dude, that cop totally knows you're Spider-Man.

What are you going to do?

You can't let her think you're Spider-Man.

She already thinks it, Gwen. There's not much he can do.

He didn't deny it, MJ. He just stared at her.

This was the mistake Peter Parker made.

Too many people knew and eventually the wrong person finds out.

Too many people ended up knowing who he was.

Who knows what kind of person she is?

What are you going to do?

Hey!!

You, lady!

Is there something you want to tell me?

You're wrong.

I'm not who you think I am.

Then I'm wrong.

Except I'm not.

There is a monster killing people out on the street!!

And--and--and you walk into my house and accuse me--

You want me to what? To prove it?

I'm a police detective and I used to be an agent of S.H.I.E.L.D.!

How long you think it will take me to frisk you and find your mask?

You--you can't just...

I know you're hurting. I know you're upset.

I know you don't know what's going on here so let me give you some advice--

We gotta 616!!

We have 616!! 616 at Brooklyn General!!

What is it??

That thing-- that thing that was here went there!!

That thing is tearing up the hospital right now!!

They called it in!!

All units.

Is that-- is that where they took my father?

You'll get there faster than we will.

WHAM

ZZAATT

SMACK

I hit him with all of the Venom blast I have.

What does it take to knock this--??

WHAM

ZZAATT

ZZAATT

Huarfrghh!

Nyaaarrghh!

There you go.

BAM BAM BAM

Get your hands off him!!

CRASH

Mom!

Get out of here!!

Are you crazy?? Get out!!

Get out of here beforRRRMMM!!

Feeeedd!

CLICK CLICK CLICK

No...

Nnooo!!

Naaarrrgghh!!

BAMBAMBAMBAM BAMBAMBAM

Police!!

DOWN NOW!!

Aaaiiee!!

New York PD!!

If you can hear my voice, evacuate this building immediately!!

I have no idea.

What the--

BAMBAMBAMBAMBAMBAMBAMBAMBAMBAMBAM

SPLAT   SPLAT   SPLAT

Come on, let's get out of--

His name was *Dr. Conrad Marcus.*

Reports are already coming in that this divorced doctor of biochemistry is, or I should say was, on staff at the research and development division of the Roxxon Corporation.

We are still waiting for official word from Roxxon as to what they know about this man and how this has all come to pass...

Was Marcus' violent mutation some sort of experiment or accident gone wrong?

Police have yet to officially confirm that Marcus is responsible for the numerous deaths associated with this "Venom monster."

You will inform the media that the Roxxon Corporation is working with authorities in all capacities so that this terrible tragedy can be put behind us.

Mr. Roxxon, a--are we working with-- I mean--

With police?

Police are downplaying reports that this new Spider-Man personally knew...

What we are doing is making sure that no one can connect what happened tonight to what's happening here.

What we are doing is waiting until this all blows over and then we will find out exactly what this @#$@# Marcus was doing with the symbiote in the first place.

What we are going to do is wait until no one is watching us... and when I give the word I want to find out how Spider-Man *became* Spider-Man and why *we can't figure out how to make a Spider-Man for ourselves!!*

Spider-Man.

Mm.

Mom?

Oh, uh...

Hey, buddy...

The End.